Secrets of an Interview

ISBN: 1-4565-0494-0
ISBN-13: 9781456504946

Secrets of an Interview

The Difference Between a Good Interview and a Great Interview: What every job seeker should know

Byron S. Nakagawa

2011

Contents

"Always bear in mind that your own resolution to succeed is more important than any other."

Abraham Lincoln

Acknowledgments

A sincere thanks to a number of individuals whose help has made this publication a reality. Foremost, thank you to my better half, this book would not be a reality without her. A special thanks to contributing editor Gloria Cockrell and to Terri Zelasko for their ideas and feedback.

Thank you Meg Nakagawa for your support, Jon Santucci for your guidance and Don Santucci for your encouragement. I am much obliged to my business partner, Scott Stockton, for helping move me closer to my dreams. Finally, thanks to the team at Create Space for putting the finishing touches on this process.

Byron Nakagawa

Introduction

Having been in the corporate workplace for over twenty years, in various capacities and in various positions of management, this book is a practical compilation of information for individuals looking to create opportunities at formal and informal interviews.

For ten of my years in corporate environments, I specifically served as a manager at several Fortune 500 companies where a structured and formalized interview process was the norm. My experience includes the management of retail stores, service establishments and technology companies.

All in all, I share my background experience to assure you that I have been on both sides of the interview process. I know how it feels to be the interviewee and I know what it is to be the interviewer. I know what interviewers are looking for and I absolutely know what employers want.

The material you are about to review is the equivalent of many years of experience, as the contributions in this book have been gathered from educators, executives and entrepreneurs. Additionally, this book has been reviewed by others who have been in human resource positions where employee hiring decisions were made. In total, if you added the number of years of experience that the book's contributors have, there's over a hundred years of experience here, at your fingertips.

More importantly, the advice here is practical and easy to use. You will not need another book on interviews, the tips you'll learn here won't be found anywhere else.

"*You may never know what results come to your action, but if you do nothing there will be no results.*"

Mahatma Gandhi

Chapter I
It's all in your mind...

Mind Set & State of Mind

Every day is an interview.

You must keep this realization in your mind daily and consistently, whether you are a student pursuing a high school diploma, an undergraduate college degree; or whether you are working an hourly shift at Subway, holding a salaried position at The Home Depot. For every individual, there is another person, someone, somewhere, that is taking notice and inventory of your strengths, your weaknesses and your work ethic.

Realistically, on a daily basis, we judge, analyze and evaluate the people around us.

The same is, of course, true for every person that we meet and have contact with. Everyone we come in contact with is, to one extent or another, watching, evaluating and making a judgment about us, about you. This reality helps us understand that the way I interact with people on a day-to-day basis stays with them and affects their mental picture of me. The way *you* interact with people on a day-to-day basis stays with them and affects their mental picture of *you*.

This judgment process happens almost immediately and can develop over time into an overall impression, or mental picture, about you. You may have met people that have "heard a lot about you" and sometimes say things like, "you look different than what I imagined you'd look like." This is because everyone develops impressions that form mental images and these mental pictures can precede you, follow you, and haunt you—in good and bad ways that you might never know.

As an example, let's take a look at someone who resides in the mentality of most Americans when they think about the civil rights movement, someone that is often discussed during our nation's recognition of Martin Luther King, Jr. Day....

Who would have thought that one act by a young lady on December Ist 1955 would ring through history and would be spoken about even today? Her refusal to give up her seat in the face of segregation was her way of taking a stand for equality. She may not have thought herself one, but she is considered a hero in the civil liberties movement. Who was that young lady? Rosa Parks. What is your mental picture of Rosa Parks? Do you have one, despite never having met her? If you learned about her in elementary school, if you've read about her through history books, if you've heard her story through documentaries on television then you indeed *do* have a mental image of Rosa Parks, even though you've probably never met her.

Rosa Parks shows us that every action causes a reaction and our actions can cause effects that outrun, outdo and outlast us. Watch what you do and say so that the mental images you leave in people's minds are positive. Our actions and especially our words can either create a world beyond our wildest dreams or can break and destroy us. It's up to you, to each his own; which will it be? Will you choose daily to be seen in a positive light? Choose your actions, reactions and words carefully because every day, you're on an interview.

Who is interviewing you? That's the million dollar question. Let's think about who is "interviewing" us within and among our lives. ...

We all live very busy lives; we're all involved in many different activities. We work, we volunteer at the boys and girls club, we attend our local church, we provide for the city mission, we purchase cookies from the girl scouts, popcorn from the boy scouts; we serve on our school board, in the PTA, on sports teams, the list goes on and on. Within our endless activities, we rub shoulders with a variety of individuals.

Who are these people that you are rubbing shoulders with? They may, in the near or distant future, be very important and influential in your life. While you get to know them, know that *they* are the ones that are watching, evaluating and analyzing you in the same way that you watch, evaluate and analyze them.

The key to making the most of these every day interviews is focusing on your approach. How do we focus on maintaining a positive reflection of ourselves in light of the realization that we're always on a potential interview?

Develop behaviors and habits that will carry you through any interview, formal or not.

This book will walk through the secrets of an interview, any interview; be it the daily and casual interview, the actual employment interview, or the promotional interview that happens over time at the job we're already performing.

To provide perspective and practical advice, we will also look at standards of dress, the hiring process and the screening process many companies utilize when selecting a candidate for hire. Although these topics will be covered separately, this book will bring them together to help you realize your potential and experience regular success, whether you know you're on an interview or not.

"The only man who makes no mistakes is the man who does nothing."

Theodore Roosevelt

Chapter 2
It's all up to you...

Would you like to know the secret to having your dream job? What would it be like to wake up every day and actually feel excited to go to work?

Do you want to feel fulfilled in your job? What would it look like, to you, to know that you are making a difference in your career?

These are the questions that people long to have answered and fulfilled in their lives. All of us look for meaning in what we are doing. What are you doing? Are you making a difference? Do you have a dream job? If your answer is no, then what are you doing to get it?

These are the questions that most individuals want answered but can't, for one reason or another, answer for themselves. Before moving forward in this book, take a moment to answer the following questions about your goals and future career and/or employment aspirations:

What are your current employment duties and/or responsibilities?

_____

_____

_____

_____

Are you good at your job?

_____

_____

_____

_____

Why do you think you are/are not?

_____

_____

_____

_____

Do you want to remain in your current employment field?

For example, if you work at a department store, do you wish to stay in sales? If you work at an insurance company, do you want to continue to work in the insurance industry?

_____

_____

If you could have a different position at your current or most recent place of employment, what would it be and why?

_____

_____

_____

_____

Do you have an interest in a field of work that is completely different than your current one?

_____

What is your interest?

_____

_____

_____

_____

Does your area of interest have a specific job that you're after?

_____

_____

_____

_____

If you can't address the questions above, can you answer this:

Do you have a dream job?

_____

What is it?

_____

_____

_____

_____

If you can't name your dream job, maybe you don't know what your dream job is. It would benefit you to think about your interests, experience and the realistic lifestyle you want to pursue.

I'd encourage you to talk to people in the fields of work that interest you so that you can seek out your dream job and go after it. Talking to individuals in your field of interest can give you insight into their respective professions and help you decide if your dream job is really a dream come true at all.

For instance, many individuals think they'd love to be a lawyer. But they don't know any lawyers, they don't have a sense of what lawyers do on a day to day basis, and they don't realize the long hours, high stress, and academic requirements of the job. A 2007 *Lifestyle* online article read that, "Dentists may have the highest rate of suicide out of any profession in the world, but attorneys have the most alcoholics out of any profession." Perhaps some real life research into the profession, before deciding to become a lawyer, may have saved one or two of them from a career they didn't enjoy enough to stay sober in.

The point is, make the most of the people around you and find out what they do so that you can find help in deciding what kind of work you'd really like to do.

Once you have narrowed down your *target* career path, then you can put into practice the interview success tools presented throughout this book.

"Nothing is more expensive than missed opportunity"

H. Jackson Brown, Jr.

Chapter 3
It's all about risk...

Missed Opportunities

We already know that every day we meet people of all walks of life, every one of them with their own story. We've talked about how busy we are and can see that American society, on a whole, thrives on overscheduled lives. We individually have our own worries, our own day, our own bills, our own families, employment obligations...many even worry about our worries and schedule time to talk to strangers about our concerns. We get so caught up with our lives that we close our eyes to the wide world of possibilities around us.

If we'd only stop, take a deep breath and open our mind, we'd see that everyone has something to offer. And we'd see that we have much to offer in return.

Know that you are no less than the person next to you. You matter and your experience is valuable. You are an asset and can contribute in a positive way. Make the choice to recognize that opportunity is staring you right in the eyes, and it's just a matter of grabbing hold of it.

What is that opportunity? It's likely the very opportunity you have been looking for, the one you wrote about at the end of Chapter 2.

Once we know what we *want*, we can begin the search to attain it and identify the opportunities in our lives that will help us reach our goals. Once we go through life with the *expectation* of opportunity, then we'll be more likely to identify the opportunities that come our way. For instance, if you are looking for a certain job, a certain amount of monetary compensation in your job, or simply desiring work that commands dignity, security, respect; know what you want and start looking for existing ways to attain those goals. Too many times people complain about the lack of opportunities today. They talk about the lack of jobs, the lack of advancement opportunities, the lack of work that is fulfilling to them. But if they'd open their eyes and ears, they'd soon hear of business owners, hiring managers, executives and non-profit employment organizations complaining that they can't find enough people to hire. Now which is it? There cannot be no people to hire and no jobs at the same time. This double negative just can't co-exist; it is an either/or situation.

The true answer for each of us is that we must not only decide what we want and look for opportunities in our lives; we must also *make* opportunities.

Go back to your own life. Evaluate, analyze and judge those around you and with whom you rub shoulders. You know more people than you realize and there are real opportunities in the circle of friends and acquaintances that you have. Be open to what kinds of doors others can open for you once you get to know them and learn more about what they do.

Do you feel it's impossible to look at your life and find opportunity? Do you feel that you just don't know anybody that can help open a door for you? What about people that come to the United States and really don't have a life or friends and acquaintances here? Why is that many newcomers to America arrive with cents in their pockets and find more opportunity and more wealth in less time than we Americans do, in spite of the fact that we are born here and can access the many opportunities here? It's because they come with an expectation that they'll find opportunity in America, and so they do and they succeed in doing so.

There is no reason to be afraid of the people you already know; do not be afraid to deepen your friendships and acquaintances and find out about people already in your own life. Getting to know your son's little league coach or your favorite grocery store's bag employee may be the first step towards landing your dream job.

"Attitude is a little thing that makes a big difference."

Winston Churchill

Chapter 4
It's all about common sense…

Everyday Casual Interviews

Let's discuss one of the most common types of interviews; the everyday, casual interview. This kind of interview happens all around us almost all of the time. The casual interview is obviously not the formal, scheduled interview nor is it one we necessarily prepare for with research; however, even the everyday casual interview can result in a dream job.

In any interview, we almost never know who we're really talking to. We don't know who the interviewers know and often don't know what they really do. All too often we assume we know to whom we are speaking, but do we really know what we're walking into? Because we don't always know who our interviewers are and what their employment role may be, it's important to go back to the principles reviewed at the beginning of this book and focus on presenting yourself in the most positive way that you can. Let's look at some examples of casual interviews, in this and the next chapter, and you'll see what I mean.

No. 1: Another One Bites the Dust
Bad Attitudes Have Big Impacts

A young man named John worked for a local grocery store. He bagged groceries and did his job well; no one had ever complained about him. On one particular day he was bagging groceries for an older gentleman that was purchasing many items. The gentleman saw how hard John was working and smiled at him, as if to say, "I see how hard you're working and I appreciate it." John returned a quick smile and continued to bag the groceries. Then the gentleman said to him, "Great weather we're having today, wouldn't you say?" John wasn't really in the mood to strike up a conversation so he simply replied, "Yeah."

"Did you see the game last night?" the man continued.

"No," John replied curtly.

"Are you a football fan?" the gentleman asked, trying to find common ground.

"Not really; here's your groceries," John said in a negative tone. John thought to himself, "*Why* is this man trying to talk to me?"

While John was typically friendly with his customers and was happy to engage them in conversation, today he had a lot on his mind. In fact, John was very anxious to get out of work on time, and he was bagging the gentleman's groceries just fifteen minutes before the end of his shift. You see, John had an interview the next day for a "real" job. He was very excited about the opportunity to leave the grocery store once and for all. He was so excited that he could hardly sleep that night.

The next morning, John got out of bed early to make sure that he would have enough time to get his clothes ironed and his face shaved. He printed out additional copies of his resume. He also left early to avoid traffic problems that would cause him to be late. He arrived early for his interview, checked in with the receptionist, and anxiously waited.

The receptionist picked up the phone to let the interviewer know that John had arrived. John was feeling exceptionally confident, having arrived early in an effort to make a positive impression. He waited patiently.

Just five minutes had passed, but John felt that he had been sitting in the reception area for an hour. At last the receptionist said, "John, Mr. Smith will see you now, please follow me."

Excited and anxious, John had a great big smile on his face as he was led down the hall. The receptionist knocked on the door, opened it and said "Mr. Smith, this is John, your 9:00AM interview." John walked from behind the receptionist, entered the office and lost his smile. Behind the desk sat Mr. Smith, who stood to greet him. As they made eye contact, John's heart sank. Mr. Smith was the man at the grocery store the day before, the gentleman that had tried to make conversation with John when he was too busy to be bothered with small talk. Now, do you think John will get that job? What if he does a stellar job during the interview? Can he salvage the opportunity?

Mr. Smith *knows* what John is really like when he's outside the parameters of a job interview. If customer service is important to Mr. Smith, and customer service is often important to most employers, Mr. Smith will remember that John couldn't be bothered to speak with him. It's infinitely more likely that John's dismissive approach is one that Mr. Smith certainly does not want his customers and clients exposed to. Seeing how John treated him shows him how John will treat new customers and John will have failed his interview, not realizing that it was happening even before he left his grocery store job. Unfortunately for John, these type of events happen almost everyday.

Every business owner, every regional manager, every corporate executive, every person in a position to hire an employee, is, at one point or another, a customer. These individuals, individuals that can offer you a career path, a benefit package, a bright future and steady income, are *always* looking for quality people that will *better* their business, *better* their company and *better* their customer and/or consumer base. Are you someone that can offer **better** to an employer? People, employers especially, want to receive outstanding service, and they want their own employees to make the consumer feel that their place, their business, their organization is willing to go the extra mile. This kind of attitude in an individual is too good to pass up.

Think that you can't carry an attitude worth hiring? Think that you don't work somewhere that a hiring party would take notice of you? Think again. You'll see why as we consider a scenario involving an individual with a *positive* attitude, who makes unexpected and unlikely opportunities.

"When we do the best that we can, we never know what miracle is wrought in our life, or in the life of another."

Helen Keller

Chapter 5
It's all about initiative...

Self-Made Opportunity

No. 2: Giving In Spite Of...
Good Attitudes Have Bigger Impacts

Joann was a hard worker, employed as a waitress, part-time, at a local restaurant while she finished her bachelors of business. Like many full-time students working part-time to put themselves through school, her life was hectic. Joann went from an eight-hour day of school to three and four hours of homework to working a five hour night shift.

But Joann was focused in school, focused at work, and determined to keep complaints out of her daily routine. While she certainly felt tired and didn't always like being in her life, she made it a point to avoid complaining and knew better than to blame anyone for her crazy schedule and its circumstances. And in fact, by merely making it a goal to avoid complaints, she found that she developed a positive attitude in the midst of her exhaustion and could meet unexpected challenges with appreciation, seeing them as new and once-in-a-lifetime opportunities. After all, school would be over soon and then some kind of "normal" life would begin for her; why waste time that was passing quickly anyway, right?

Described positively by customers, Joann is seen as "a highly attentive server with a smile on her face and a bounce in her step." Joann always looked for ways to create a delightful dining experience for each of her customers.

After a long day at school and what seemed to be harder than usual homework assignments, Joann headed off to work as usual. She was really tired this day, and it seemed really hard to put that smile on her face. Then it seemed that her customers were more irritable than normal. Finally, she thought she'd had it when she was assigned to serve a middle-aged couple.

Joann cheerfully greeted them and explained the specials; she then offered them something to drink. Right from the start, the man was a piece of work. "Aren't you going to give me some time to look at the menu before you start bothering us about a drink?" Even if she had been taken aback, Joann responded with, "Ok, I can give you a few moments. If you like

I can make some suggestions, and if you look right here on the menu, you will find our drink selections." She knew right away that this was not going to be an easy table to serve. As the evening and their dinner progressed she made certain to go out of her way to make sure that their drinks were always full; she also made sure she gave quality suggestions and answered any questions they had. Slowly but surely by the end of the night the man had changed due to Joann's commitment to only give outstanding service, no matter the circumstance. As she wrapped up the night with this couple she asked them if there was anything else she could do or get for them. The man that was upset from the beginning said, "Yes, there is one more thing." "Ok," Joann replied, not really sure what to expect. The man reached in his pocket and said, "I apologize for being in such a sour mood. I own a company and we have been having some trouble with a merger, not that any of that is your concern. But you gave me profound service despite my attitude…thank you." Joann heard him say that she was a great people person, had a great attitude and excellent work ethic.…. She took his card as he finished saying, "I would love to talk to you more about a position at my company." Blown away Joann said thank you and took his card.

And so Joann set up an interview and was offered a position with the company. Not only did she receive a major pay increase but the owner of the company determined that, to keep her as an employee, he needed to help her take advantage of the company's benefit program, which in-

cluded assistance with tuition re-imburse-
ment for graduate programs.

Things rarely are what they appear.
The person you meet tomorrow could
have a profound impact on your life and
may even change your life forever. Even if
the story above seems improbable to you,
you'd be surprised how often things happen just like that. A cashier at McDon-
ald's gets offered a position at a perfume
counter because she smiles and remem-
bers the customer's name. A personal fit-
ness trainer gets offered a sales spot on the
floor of a premiere dealership because he's
great with his clients and knows how to
sell himself. These opportunities might
not come with a health plan or tuition
reimbursement, but they're a step up on
the ladder of someone's career, someone's

dream job. Could that someone be you? Of course it can!

Just always remember that executives, business owners and managers keep their eyes open for people with great attitudes and great work ethic. And you can't always spot that executive, hiring manager or human resource director at the airport counter, in the seat next to you at the theater, or in the check out line.

A very successful business owner once told me, "I can teach anyone practically anything, but I can't teach a person to have a good attitude, and I don't have time to teach work ethic." Employers are always on the look-out for people like Joann. Make the choice to be someone caught in acts of excellence. Why? Because people are always watching you and always taking a mental snapshot that stays with them.

"The key to nailing a good interview is to be smart enough for the job, but dumb enough not to intimidate the interviewer."

Michael Haynes

Chapter 6
It's all about putting the best foot forward…

First Impressions

No doubt you've heard that a first impression is everything. Maybe you think you get this concept and that you're ok with it. Maybe you think you know how to make a good first impression.

But even the simplest concepts can make a difference, so DO NOT UNDER ESTIMATE the significance of the following information…

Dress for Success. What should you wear to the interview? First and foremost, don't be fooled by employees that already work at the place of employment you want to enter; it is always better to be overdressed than it is to be underdressed.

If you're reading this and think this is a "no-brainer," think again. Truth-be told, if everyone *did* know this, I would not be writing about it.

At minimum, acceptable clothing for men and women is always business casual. It doesn't matter if you are interviewing at McDonalds, Bank of America, at the Home Deport or Petsmart—***don't*** show up at an interview in shorts or jeans and a t-shirt.

What is business casual for men? Khaki pants that are clean, not torn, and starched. You don't have to have pleats, but don't pull these off the floor, no matter what name brand they are. It's best to go with slacks, and if your slacks have a print or pattern on them, you'll need the matching suit jacket, or don't wear them.

Men need to wear a buttoned shirt that has a collar. This does not include a polo shirt. While a tie is not typically included in business casual dress, men should always have a strong tie that compliments them and that can be worn with the typical collared shirt which is usually white, blue or gray in a business setting.

What about women? At minimum, women need to wear a blouse, i.e., a collared shirt, with either a skirt or slacks. While women tend to have more options when it comes to business casual clothes, the collared shirt is best unless she can find a sharp sweater set or a sheath dress suit. Skirts always need to be knee length, at least, and stockings need to be worn, along with professional shoes, no matter the season or temperature. Professional shoes are not always at the height of fashion, but you don't want your business employer to be distracted during the interview and you want to make the impression that you are both reasonable and responsible. This means that men need to wear some type of dress shoe as well, no tennis shoes, sneakers or sports shoes.

Additionally, men should have a modest hair cut, no mohawks, no colored hair. Men with long hair should pull it back or cut it to above the collar. Women with longer hair should avoid loud hairstyles and should consider putting their hair up so as, again, not to be distracting during the interview.

If you are going to wear perfume or cologne to your interview, or at all, do not apply too much as it may not be a desirable smell for the interviewer. Practice regular hygiene, wear deodorant, brush your teeth and make sure that your clothes, hair and skin are not carrying problematic smells, like cigarette smoke, or articles, such as pet hair.

Many companies do not have large areas for interviews, which means you may be in close quarters with your interviewers. Make sure your breath is fresh! Eat a mint or use mouthwash before you walk into your interview.

Men should be neatly shaved or have their facial hair trimmed closely, and women should avoid large earrings and excessive jewelry. In an interview, *less is more*. Both men and women should be aware of this simple truth.

For individuals specifically advised to dress in "professional" attire, and not business casual attire, please take this seriously. In these cases, both men and women should dress in a professional, well-fitting, dark suit and wear a light, but not brightly colored, collared, button-down shirt with long sleeves.

There are certain employment fields where it is always best to dress in professional attire, even if the interviewer does not specifically request that you do so. These include pharmaceutical sales positions, medical offices, law firms, and corporate offices. If you are scheduled for a formal interview, try to visit the office on a weekday, not Friday where casual dress may be allowed, so that you can see what kind of dress is generally expected and make sure to meet the minimum expectations. Use your best judgment in all instances and remember that it's always best to be over-dressed, than under-dressed.

"To be prepared is half the victory."
Miguel de Cervantes

Chapter 7
It's all about preparation...

Know Your Interviewer

When you're called to attend a job interview, setting the date and time is just the first step. Prepare yourself to outshine all the other candidates. How?

There are several steps to ensure that you are ahead of other candidates, even before you walk in the door. First, we live in an information age so research the company online, and if you are able, talk to people already employed by the company, person or organization you want to work for. If you do not have online access at home, plan ahead and do your research at a public library. Your interviewer may not necessarily ask what you know about the company, but if they do, you'll need to be ready.

Even more important is the fact that, in learning about the company, person or organization, you may decide that it's not a good fit for you. Your future employer has to sell the job to you just as much as you have to sell yourself. Be diligent in learning about your future employer because you never know where things might lead in your career path. What you find out may change your mind or solidify your goals concerning employment.

Finally, always take a copy of your updated resume even if you have had no previous work experience. Everyone, everyone, everyone has a resume, which is sometimes referred to as a curriculum vitae (CV) in the business and/or medical field.

A resume is an overview of an individual's activities, experience and qualifications. The experience included can refer to employment experience, volunteer experience, academic experience, etc. Your resume depends on you.

For instance, we are all, at one time or another, a part of various groups and organizations that provide us with unique skills and experiences. For instance, a first-time job applicant may have been a member of the Boy Scouts and can point to different leadership training and skills that may be applicable to the job. A Boy Scout can likely ask his Troop Leader to serve as a job reference. He can describe experiences where he's had to work as a member of a team and may even have examples of times when he served as a leader himself.

Often, we are all a part of a group or activity-based membership such as the Boy Scouts or Girl Scouts, church groups, non-profit groups, school or after-school activities, and so on and so forth, the list goes on.

Compile your resume and then aim to always have a resume on hand. At formal job interviews, be sure to bring a few extra copies of your resume to the interview, even if you submitted it to the employer ahead of time. Do this so that, if your resume was misplaced, or if for some reason it was not given to your interviewer, she can have it readily available and speak to you about it. She will greatly appreciate it.

"At the center of your being you have the answer; you know who you are and you know what you want."

Lao Tzu

Chapter 8
It's all about the truth...

Know the Answers

In almost every interview, there are a series of questions that begin the process. Prepare yourself to answer a list of standard questions set forth here, and do your best to become familiar with your answers so that they are given with ease. Thinking through your answers and practicing your responses may seem silly, but it will help with nervousness and forgetfulness that can occur during the interview itself.

Most standard interviewers will begin with:

Tell me about yourself

_____

_____

_____

_____

_____ and will ask:

*Why do you want to work here?*_____ _____

_____

_____

_____

_____

_____

_____

This question requires research. Research the company/organization website and, if you can, talk to someone already employed there about the job, its requirements, its challenges, its benefits, etc. Unless you've given it some thought, it may be a challenge to answer the question of: *Why should I hire you?*

_____

_____

_____

_____

What are your strengths? Or

Tell me about your three greatest strengths is a popular question and, if possible, your answers should relate to the job itself.

_____

_____

_____

_____

_____

_____

_____

_____

Now let's pause for a second and spend some time on this next question: *What are your weaknesses?*

This question is often hard to answer in a positive way. You need to be honest in answering this question. Think about your answer and practice it out loud, perhaps with someone who knows you well and can tell you if the answer sounds real.

For instance, if procrastination is your weakness, you can say that you sometimes have problems prioritizing your work.

If this is the case for you, perhaps you could explain that, once you realized your weakness, you were able to go to a previous manage/employer and, having told them that you had problems with "getting things done on time," they suggested using or creating a calendar or task system to make sure you met deadlines.

This does a couple of things for you. You have presented your weakness without it being a liability. You have shown that you have improved on this weakness. Make sure that the employer sees that you are self-aware and that you are looking to continue to improve, in spite of your weaknesses. Also, it shows that you are open to feedback and can make changes on the job when required.

So tackle this one head-on: What are some of your weaknesses?

_____

_____

_____

_____

_____

Another challenging and often-asked question is: *What do you think you will bring to our company that is unique?* Or: *What can you offer our organization?*

_____

_____

_____

_____

_____

If you're seeking a position with a national or international organization, expect questions like: Can you describe a time/setting where you had to work with people from another culture? How did you react and how did this make you feel?

_____

_____

_____

_____

_____

_____

Or something along the lines of: When you are in a setting with people from another culture that differs from yours, are you able to adapt? Can you give me an example of this?_____

_____

_____

_____

_____

_____

Some questions are specifically geared to gauge your temperament and/or your personality. Think of honest examples and practice your answers with someone who knows you or has worked with you in the past.

For instance:

Can you tell me about a time when you did not agree with another employee?

What was the situation and what was the end result?_____

_____

_____

_____

_____

No job is perfect, can you tell me about a time when you saw a process that was either unnecessary or not efficient and what you did to improve this?

_____

_____

_____

_____

_____

_____

These are just a few of the questions that you may be asked. I highly encourage you to take the time to fill in the blanks for these questions, practice them aloud and memorize your answers. They may seem like questions that are easy to understand, but they can be difficult to answer during your interview.

"The cost of a thing is the amount of what I will call life, which is required to be exchanged for it, immediately or in the long run."

Henry David Thoreau

Chapter 9
It's all about worth…

The Cost of Hiring

If you skipped the questions in the previous chapter, go back and take them seriously. Yes, it's completely normal to wonder *why* some of those questions are asked, but be careful not to get caught up in the wondering of why and why you should have to convince your interviewer to hire you. The reality is, you are trying to convince strangers to give you, over every other applicant, an opportunity that you don't actually or exactly or sometimes even remotely know anything about!

Sure, you might have a solid understanding of the job, but until you actually *have* the job, there's no way for you or your interviewer to know if you can do it and if you can do it well. More importantly, if you're not prepared to present yourself well, the interview might just do a cost-value analysis and decide that you are not a good investment. What do I mean by "investment"? Let me explain.

The vast majority of us do not take into careful consideration what companies pay to hire, train and retain their employees. As a manager at several Fortune 500 Companies throughout my career, it was my job to make sure new employees were properly trained and adequately capable of the training.

When overseeing new-hire employees, managers know they need to give them room for error, but mistakes cost money and new employees who are prone to mistakes early on are not a good investment for the hiring company. Training someone takes time and energy. That time and energy, expended on the new hire, is time and energy that is not yet being used for the benefit of the company. So the <u>cost</u> of hiring, training and retaining a valuable and well-trained employee is something that is taken very seriously by every company, association, organization and business.

Why all the talk about cost? Because it's something that hiring managers understand and consider when they're deciding to fill an employment position. Often, if you do not understand the cost of a company's hiring process, it will be hard <u>not</u> to take a job for granted.

Realize that companies pour thousands of dollars into advertising when trying to hire employees. They pay for market research to find the most suitable ways to attract the people they would like to hire. Then they pay individuals, like the salaried human resource manager and her team, to conduct initial interviews, screen potential hires and interview future employees. Typically, employment candidates must meet certain criteria before a salaried manager will get involved in the hiring process. But once a new person is hired, either a member from the company's Human Resources group or the corporation's training team, will have to conduct initial training. Once the costly and time-consuming process of training is complete, a supervising manager becomes a part of the new hire's experience and oversees the actual <u>job</u> training of the new employee. When you consider the cost expended to actually prepare the person for the job, the relevant cost to hire ratio can be an overwhelming figure.

I can personally attest to this ratio, having worked at one Fortune 500 company that spends $65,000, yes, sixty-five thousand dollars, to hire and train one employee that earns $28,000 (twenty-eight thousand dollars) a year. This means that the hiring company spends almost two and a half times the person's annual income just to hire him! And this is done with absolutely no guarantee as to how long that employee will stay with the hiring organization. This is why employers are so selective and this is why you need to make an exceptionally good impression of yourself. Employers don't just want a "good" employee. They need and require longevity, commitment, and a good foundation of skills, attitude and/or enthusiasm in order to break even or seek to profit from hiring you.

"The real art of conversation is not only to say the right thing at the right place but to leave unsaid the wrong thing at the tempting moment."

Dorothy Nevill

Chapter 10
It's all about staying alert...

What Not to Say

In every interview, and in many casual interview situations, someone inevitably asks you what you did _not_ like about a previous job.

PLEASE note: this is not the time or place to get on a soapbox about all the wrong doings concerning your previous organization, group, business or company. What an interviewer is looking for is your attitude and your ability to be a good reflection of an organization, group, business or company. In short, the interviewer really wants to know if you are or are going to be a _complainer_. It's important to know if you are going to be a "cancer" among current employees by bringing a negative or bad attitude to the workplace.

Additionally, the interviewer wants to know if you will be a good fit for the open position. For instance, are there experiences, situations or responsibilities from your previous job that you did not like or that you found boring? Are those tasks or work procedures going to be similar to the ones that accompany the job you are applying for? Don't risk it!

While you may not have liked a particular aspect or duty of your previous job, make sure that you convey your responses in a positive light. You can certainly indicate that something was not to your liking, but be sure that you convey it in such a way that tells the interviewer that you were willing to do the job and to do it well, even if you didn't always like it. All the talk about attitude in the previous chapters comes into play during the casual interview and again during the formal interview.

As you did with previous questions, practice answering questions about why you left a certain position or term of employment. Honesty is always the best policy, but you don't want to take yourself out of the candidate pool. For example, perhaps you were in a previous position where you did not like working with the customers and yet, the job you are applying for involves customer interaction on a consistent basis. You don't want to say you disliked customers, after all, your new customers might be a joy to work with! Instead, you'll want to be specific about why you left without saying negative things about your employer or your employer's "customers."

Remember that negativity will almost always cause an interviewer to assume right away that you are not the one she is looking for. Don't let a negative remark or previous bad experience demonstrate something negative about <u>you</u>. After all, you don't want to cut yourself short this time around!

"If you are prepared, you will be confident, and will do the job."

Tom Landry

Chapter II
It's all in your presentation...

Be Thoroughly Prepared

What did your 9th grade teacher always tell you to do when you were in class? Don't remember? Maybe if I mentioned a pen and notebook....

Starting in high school, it was vitally important to learn the art of *taking notes*. This very skill is a MAJOR secret when it comes to the interview process. If you take nothing else away from this book, know that it is foremost important, in your interview, to be PREPARED. *What do I mean?*

Just this: note taking is a little secret that potential employees should know about. It's something that could make the difference between you and the other candidates. If done properly, a request to take notes will WOW your interviewer and let them know that you are serious about the job.

Never heard of taking notes during an interview? Think about it, the interviewer will be taking notes, so why not you? Make sure that you ask for permission to take notes before you actually start taking notes. And be respectful of the interviewer's response.

For example, you could ask, "Would anyone mind if I take notes during the interview? It has been my experience that sometimes a question may have several parts to it and I want to make sure I answer all parts of your questions." You could also mention that taking notes helps you stay on track and that you want to make sure you provide whatever information is requested. If you can convey your request in a positive way, not only will the interviewer agree that you can take notes; your credibility with the interviewer will increase ten-fold.

Also, as you go through the interview, write down any questions that come to mind. If you have the opportunity to then ask questions of the interviewer, being able to go back to your notes shows that you are truly interested in the company and the position. Finally, taking notes can also serve to help you make an informed decision when you are deciding if you want to take the job.

"Sometimes questions are more important than answers."

Nancy Willard

Chapter 12

What do you want to know before you walk out the door?

Asking Questions of Your Interviewer

At the end of your interview, most interviewers will ask if you have any questions for them. This is not your time to be shy; take advantage of this opportunity. Most interviewees assume that, by *not* asking questions, they are showing their intelligence and that they have an understanding about the job. This perception couldn't be further from the truth.

Naturally, you do not want to over-load the interviewer with too many questions and you don't want to ask questions that are overtly simple or obvious; however, you do want to ask two or three well thought-out questions that concern the specific position or an aspect of the company that will directly affect the job.

For example, many interviewers will provide a brief description of the position's duties and/or responsibilities. If, at the close of the interview, you then ask, "Now, what would my responsibilities entail?" Well, needless to say, this would **<u>not</u>** be a good question in light of the fact that the information was already covered. Asking an obvious question like that only serves to give the impression that you did not listen to the interviewer or that you did not understand the interviewer. In either case, you will not succeed in making a good first impression. Even worse, asking an obvious question concerning information already provided affects your credibility and only shows that you are not able to make a simple connection between information about the job and comprehension about the job's duties.

Taking the time to ask questions also provides the place for you to take advantage of one of the biggest secrets of successful interviewing—taking time to ask questions allows you to effectively _ask for the job_.

Your interviewer isn't likely to come right out and tell you that she wants you to ask for the job. Not many people know to do this.

Yes, in your interview, in your own way, _ask_ for the job. You're there for a job that is offered, getting the interview means that the hiring company or organization has some interest in you, so why not ask for the opportunity that is being offered? Believe it or not, many interviewers even want you to.

Here is a list of some quality questions that will show true interest in the job, real intelligence, and a genuine desire for long-term growth with the company, business or organization in question.

Questions for the Interviewer

1. Are there opportunities for advancement in this department (or office in which you are seeking employment)?

2. Will there be a probation period for the position? What are some of the goals that you'll expect of

me within the first 90 days? (or six
months; within the first year, etc.)

3. Is there a formal mentoring program? *Or,* is there opportunity
to be matched or assigned with a
mentor that can help in my training?

These are just a few examples of good
questions to ask. While every person's
personality is different, your job is to find
the questions that fit your situation, tailor
them to you and to the position you seek.
I highly recommend that you write down
your questions in advance of the interview
and take them with you when you go to
your interview.

If you have a position, organization
or business in mind, take some time here
to write down three to four of your own
questions.

1._____

_____

_____

_____

2._____

_____

_____

_____

_____

_____

_____

_____

3._____

_____

_____

_____

_____

_____

_____

_____

_____

4._____

_____

_____

_____

_____

_____

_____

_____

"Beware of the person who can't be bothered by details."

Willim Feather

Chapter 13
It's all in the details...

Additional Tips

Common Sense Strategies

- Always leave early for your interview.

You never know if you'll run into a traffic jam, an accident or a need for additional directions while on your way. If you take the extra time, you will arrive early, as you should, so that the interviewer knows you will be prompt and on time for work.

How early should you arrive? Arrive, at most, fifteen minutes early. Do not arrive any earlier for your interview unless it is specifically mentioned or suggested to you. It may not make complete sense to you, but interviewers often have a number of candidates scheduled and are busy with their usual tasks; they do not appreciate individuals arriving extremely early.

During the Interview:

·   Maintain eye contact.

Consistent eye contact conveys that you are trustworthy and helps the interviewer identify with you, even like you.

·   Offer a firm handshake.

Even for women, a firm, but not hard and _not_ aggressive handshake, is something that conveys confidence.

·   Mirror the body language of your interviewer.

Be careful not to mimic the interviewer, just subtly mirror his actions or mannerisms. Mirroring your interviewer allows the interviewer to trust you, and that connection strengthens the bond between you and the interviewer.

- Smile.

Smiling is contagious and the very act of smiling affects a person's emotional state. Smiling creates a feeling of happiness, releases endorphins, and extends a positive association to you which, in turn, increases your chances of getting the job.

- Be thorough and speak intelligently. When the interviewer asks you a question and you don't know what to say, take a minute to think about the answer before speaking. For instance, if you're asked to tell the interviewer about yourself, and you're caught off guard, don't sell yourself short. Saying, "I am in school, uh that's really it," isn't going to be enough. You need to speak intelligently about what you have done in the past or what experiences you have, even if you have never been gainfully employed before.

Remember that your experiences, even those outside of employment, can make a difference. Experiences that include volunteer work, for example, provide wonderful responses to interviewers who want to know about you.

·   Try to avoid empty phrases.

Saying, "I don't know," or, "I'm not sure how to answer that," does not give your interviewers opportunity to get to know you or decide if they like you.

Empty phrases convey a lack of preparation or worse, and may even demonstrate that you have an empty personality that isn't easy to like.

"How am I going to live today in order to create the tomorrow I'm committed to?"

Anthony Robbins

Chapter 14
Leaving on a high note...

Conclusion

Now that your eyes have been opened to opportunities that surround you, hopefully, you'll see them. We've focused on changing the way you think, discussing interviews on several different levels, and walked through various steps to help you find the successful opportunity you're looking for.

So now that you've got new insight and know how to put your best foot forward, what will you do?

Remember that good intentions lead nowhere. Take the time to fill in the blanks in this book and utilize the time to get to know yourself better.

Now that you know potential interviewers can be everywhere, begin to take inventory of the people in your life. When you talk to individuals in your life or new people you meet, make mental notes as to how that individual can be a help to your future plans.

Even if you're not actively seeking a job and even if you don't have any idea when your next interview will happen, learn to step outside of your comfort zone and network with people already in your life. For those of you that know where you want to end up or what employment opportunity you want to pursue, you might be surprised to find someone in your circle of friends and acquaintances that can help you find your way. Don't be afraid to create opportunities through the individuals in your life.

Anthony Robbins puts it beautifully, stating, "In essence, if we want to direct our lives, we must take control of our consistent actions. It's not what we do once in a while that shapes our lives, but what we do consistently." So don't just think about these concepts once and decide that they do not work. Stay consistent when looking for opportunities, stay positive, and be prepared for the casual and the formal interviews.

Finally, thank your interviewer for his time and for his consideration. Leave them wanting to see you in the very job you're asking for.

Appendix

<table>
<tr><td>Local:</td><td>Permanent:</td></tr>
</table>

Local: **Permanent:**
123 Main St   200 Victor St.
Buffalo, NY 14225   Boston, MA 01234
(555)123-1234   (555)555-1234

Will B. Hired

Wbh1234@amn.edu

Objective   To obtain a co-op or internship in electrical engineering for Summer, 2011.

Education   **University of Buffalo**   University St, NY
Bachelors of Science in Electrical Engineering
Junior standing- 75 Credits Earned   **Graduating May 2012**
GPA: 3.25
Relevant courses:

Signal and image processing	Solid state Devices
Optical Fiber Communications	Linear Control Systems
Digital Integrated Circuits	Principles and Applications of Lasers
Signals and Circuits I	Electronic Circuit Design

Work   **Big Electrical Incorporated**—Rochester, NY   May 10–Aug 10
Experience   Embedded Systems Validation Group Intern
- Tested for power consumption and timing specs of ADC and DAC chips
- Validated correct functioning of transistor-level circuitry and made suggestions for sizing adjustments
- Gained a deep understanding of the design approaches for robust circuitry
- Develop a broad range of skills in oscilloscope and DMM usage, and trained other interns with the equipment
- Acquired a general understanding of the entire chips design process, from Architecture to validation and testing

Barnes and Noble—Boston, MA   May 09–Sep 09
Book seller
Old Navy—Worcester, MA   June 08–Aug 08
Sales Associate

Skills   **Software:** C++, Visual Studio, NET, HTML, Microsoft Office, Java Scripting
Hardware: VHDL, P-SPICE circuit design environment, Logic Works, circuit design and assemble, oscilloscope and DMM usage

Activities   University of Buffalo Robot club   2009–Present
& Honors   * Led a group of five students in the design of a life-size animal robot
* Won the wow award in the 2009 America loves robots contest
* Gained an in-depth knowledge of many microcontrollers
Alpha Kappa Delta- Treasurer   2008–Present
* Kept tract of the financial needs
* Organized yearly budget and expenditure reports
Big Kahuna Inc. Scholarship   2008–Present

References Available upon request

Bess Dress

---

12 Crazy Street, Spokane, WA 98543 -(123)345-6543

Qualifications Summary

Administrative Support professional experienced working in fast-paced environment demanding strong organizational, technical and interpersonal skills. Trust worthy, ethical and discreet, committed to superior customer service. Confident and poised in interactions with individuals at all levels. Detail-oriented and resourceful in completing projects; able to multi task effectively. Capabilities include:

* Customer Service & Relations
* General Accounting
* Computer Operations
* Accounts Payable/Receivable
* Telephone Reception

* Filing & Data Archiving
* Word Processing & Typing
* Problem Solving
* Office Equipment Operation

Experience Highlights

Administrative Support
*Performed administrative and secretarial support functions for the President of a large sportswear Manufacturer. Coordinated and managed multiple priorities and projects.

*Provided discreet secretarial and reception service for a busy family counseling center. Scheduled appointments and maintained accurate, up-to-date confidential client files.

* Assisted with general accounting functions, maintained journals and handled A/P and A/R, provided telephone support, investigated and resolved billing problems for an 18-member manufacturer's buying group. Trained and supervised part-time staff and interns.

Customer Service & Reception
*Registered incoming patients in a hospital emergency room. Demonstrated ability to maintain composure and work efficiently in a fast-paced environment while preserving strict confidentiality.

*Conducted patient interviews to elicit necessary information for registration, accurate, prioritization, and to assist medical professionals in the process

*Orchestrated hotel special events and reservations, managed customer relations and provided exemplary service to all customers.

Management & Supervision
*Promoted rapidly from front desk clerk to assistant front office manager at an upscale hotel. Oversaw all Operations including restaurant, housekeeping, and maintenance. Troubleshot and resolved problems, mediated staff disputes and handled customer complaints.

*Participated in staff recruitment, hiring , training and scheduling, supervised a front-desk staff.

Employment History
Accounting Assistant, Guardian, Inc., Gonic, IL
Patient Services Registrar, Kelidia Health systems Hospital, San Jose, CA
Assistant Front Office Manager, Hilton Paris, Los Angeles, CA
Receptionist / Secretary, Family counseling center, Poway, CA
Administrative Assistant, Dick sporting Goods, Long Beach CA

Bobby Jo Smith

132 Main St, Anywhere, FL 09876
(445)321-0123 • Email BJSmith@gmail com

Profile:

I am a dedicated individual who has great ambition. I have experience as a Administrative Assistant at a Insurance Agency. I'm willing to learn new things, can work under pressure. I get along with others, I can handle a challenge. I am seeking a portion where I can learn and grow as well as give my best.

Employment:

Administrative Assistant-Fred Martin Insurance Agency-18 Main St. Carlsbad, NM 01235 June 2004—Feb 2011

My title was the Director of First Impressions/Administrative Assistant. I handled multiple lines, greeted the clients as the came in, I also helped out with any tasks they gave me. I would do the monthly commission statements by imputing data in the computer, filed, faxed, scanned, mail

Administrative Assistant-Six feet under Las Cruces. NM 05412 May 2004—Jun 2004

I was the administrative assistant to the office manager. I did a lot of data entry, filed paperwork as it came in.

Education:

Alamogordo High School- 10 Miner Way Alamogordo NM 01542
High School 2000-2004

Skills:

I can handle multiple phone lines, filing, scanning, commission statements, opened, stamped and disbursed the mail as it came in.

References:

·   Furnished upon request

There are great websites to help you build your resume for free or at a low cost:

www.theresumebuilder com

www.howtowritearesume.net/resumebuilder.aspx

www.gotresumebuilder.com

www.resume-builder.net

Federal Department of Labor

www.dol.gov

You can also check out any of your state department of labor websites. They are usually set up in the following way: labor (then your state) dot gov. For example, in NY the site is: labor.ny.gov or in Idaho its labor.idaho.gov, and so on.

Sample Cover Letters:
Hard copy: sender address and contact information at top. **Your address and the date can be left-**
justified, or centered*.)*
Your Street Address
City, State Zip Code
Telephone Number
E-mail Address

Month, Day, Year

Mr./Ms./Dr. FirstName LastName
Title
Name of Organization
Street or P. O. Box Address
City, State Zip Code

Dear Mr./Ms./Dr. LastName:

Opening paragraph: State why you are writing; how you learned of the organization or position, and basic information about yourself.

2nd paragraph: Tell why you are interested in the employer or type of work the employer does (Simply stating that you are interested does not tell why, and can sound like a form letter). Demonstrate that you know enough about the employer or position to relate your background to the employer or position. Mention specific qualifications which make you a good fit for the employer's needs. (Focus on what you can do for the employer, not what the employer can do for you.) This is an opportunity to explain in more detail relevant items in your resume. Refer to the fact that your resume is enclosed. Mention other enclosures if such are required to apply for a position.

3rd paragraph: Indicate that you would like the opportunity to interview for a position or to talk with the employer to learn more about their opportunities or hiring plans. State what you will do to follow up, such as telephone the employer within two weeks. If you will be in the employer's location and could offer to schedule a visit, indicate when. State that you would be glad to provide the employer with any additional information needed. Thank the employer for her/his consideration.

Sincerely,

(Your handwritten signature [on hard copy])

Your name, typed
(In case of e-mail, your full contact information appears below your printed name [instead of at the top, as for hard copy], and there is no handwritten signature)

Enclosure(s) (refers to resume, etc.)

(Note: the contents of your letter might best be arranged into four paragraphs. Consider what you need to say and use good writing style. See the following examples for variations in organization and layout.)

E-2 Apartment Heights Dr.
Blacksburg, VA 24060
(540) 555-0101
abcd@vt.edu

February 22, 2011

Dr. Michelle Rhodes
Principal, Wolftrap Elementary School
1205 Beulah Road
Vienna, VA 22182

Dear Dr. Rhodes:

I enjoyed our conversation on February 18th at the Family and Child Development seminar on teaching elementary children and appreciated your personal input about balancing the needs of children and the community during difficult economic times. This letter is to follow-up about the Fourth Grade Teacher position as discussed at the seminar. I will complete my M.Ed. in Curriculum and Instruction at Virginia Tech in May 2011, and will be available for employment as soon as needed for the 2011-12 school year.

My teacher preparation program at Virginia Tech has included a full academic year of student teaching. Last semester I taught second grade and this semester am teaching fourth grade. These valuable experiences have afforded me the opportunity to:

Develop lesson plans on a wide range of topics and varying levels of academic ability,
Work with emotionally and physically challenged students in a total inclusion program,
Observe and participate in effective classroom management approaches,
Assist with parent-teacher conferences, and
Complete in-service sessions on diversity, math and reading skills, and community relations.

My experience includes work in a private day care facility, Rainbow Riders Childcare Center, and in Virginia Tech's Child Development Laboratory. Both these facilities are NAEYC-accredited and adhere to the highest standards. At both locations, I led small and large group activities, helped with lunches and snacks, and implemented appropriate activities. Both experiences also provided me with extensive exposure to the implementation of developmentally appropriate activities and materials.

I enthusiastically look forward to putting my knowledge and experience into practice in the public school system. Next week I will be in Vienna, and I plan to call you then to answer any questions that you may have. I can be reached before then at (540) 555-7670. Thank you very much for your consideration.

Sincerely,

(handwritten signature)
Donna Harrington

Enclosure